LONELY

First published 1990
by Cherrytree Press Ltd
Windsor Bridge Road
Bath, Avon BA2 3AX England

Copyright © Cherrytree Press Ltd 1990

First published in the United States 1991
by Raintree Publishers

Copyright © 1991 Raintree Publishers Limited Partnership

Library of Congress Number: 90-46540

1 2 3 4 5 6 7 8 9   95 94 93 92 91

Library of Congress Cataloging-in-Publication Data

Amos, Janine.
 Feelings/by Janine Amos; illustrated by Gwen Green.
 Cover title.
 Contents: [1] Afraid—[2] Angry—[3] Hurt—[4] Jealous—
[5] Lonely—[6] Sad.
 1. Emotions—Case studies—Juvenile literature. [1. Emotions.]
I. Green, Gwen, ill.   II. Title.
BF561.A515   1991
152.4—dc20   90-46540
                                                        CIP
                                                         AC

 ISBN 0-8172-3775-5 (v. 1); ISBN 0-8172-3776-3 (v. 2); ISBN
0-8172-3777-1 (v. 3); ISBN 0-8172-3778-X (v. 4); ISBN 0-8172-
3779-8 (v. 5); ISBN 0-8172-3780-1 (v. 6).

LONELY

By Janine Amos
Illustrated by Gwen Green

RAINTREE PUBLISHERS
Milwaukee

TINA'S STORY

It was Joanne's birthday party. All the kids were sitting quietly. They were watching Magic Wanda the magician and her puppet Bonzo.

"You'll all have to help with this trick," said Bonzo. "It's a new one. I may need some more practice to get it just right. You can help me by wishing hard."

Everyone helped. Most of the kids held hands and giggled with excitement. Tina was sitting by herself. She didn't hold anyone's hand. But she was wishing just as hard as the others.

The trick worked! Bonzo pulled a bunch of paper flowers out of his hat. He took a bow, and everyone clapped. It was the end of the show.

Tina watched the other kids run off to play. She started to follow them. But then she stopped.

"I can't go," she thought. "I won't know what to say." She felt left out.

"Hi! Why aren't you playing with your friends?" asked Magic Wanda. Tina didn't answer.

Why won't Tina answer?

Magic Wanda had a lot of things to put away. There were puppets, masks, scarves, and other things. Tina helped. She passed Magic Wanda her magic wand and the paper flowers. Magic Wanda put them into a big box. And all the time, Magic Wanda talked to Tina. She told her lots of funny jokes. But Tina didn't say a word.

When they had finished, Magic Wanda thanked Tina for her help.

"I used to be shy, like you," said Magic Wanda.

Tina couldn't believe it!

"I'll tell you a secret," said Magic Wanda quietly. "Bonzo has some magic especially for shy people."

As Tina watched, Magic Wanda wriggled her hand, and Bonzo came to life again.

What do you think the magic will be?

"I'll whisper," said Bonzo. Tina leaned forward to listen. "The magic is to think about other people. Try to forget about yourself—just for a minute."

"But how do you start?" asked Tina.

"You start with a question!" said Bonzo. "There's always at least one question you can ask."

"You're using the magic now," Magic Wanda said.

"What do you mean?" asked Tina.

"You're talking to me!" said Magic Wanda. "And talking to people gets easier every time you do it!"

"Just like a magic trick!" laughed Tina.

Just then, Joanne ran in from the yard. She was out of breath, and she looked happy. Tina wondered what games the others were playing outside. She started to feel left out again.

If you were Tina, what would you do now?

Just in time, Tina remembered Bonzo's magic.

"Are you having a good time, Joanne?" she asked. "What are you playing?"

"Hide-and-seek!" said Joanne. "Come on and play!" Joanne took hold of Tina's hand.

As they ran off, Tina waved to Magic Wanda.

"It works!" she called.

"Just like my magic!" said Magic Wanda.

How did Magic Wanda help? Who would you talk to if you felt left out?

Feeling like Tina

Have you ever felt left out, like Tina did? Have you ever been too shy to join in? If you have, you'll know how lonely it makes you feel. You think you're the only one who isn't having a good time.

Don't let shyness win

Shyness can stop you from doing the things you'd like to do. It can make you blush and feel afraid to speak. But try not to worry. Most people feel shy sometimes. Try to think about something else for a moment. Try to go on doing what you want to do. Don't let shyness win.

Helping yourself

You can try to find out more about other people. You can ask them questions about themselves. You can try to stop worrying about how you are feeling. It's hard at first, but practice helps.

Think About It

Read the stories in this book. Think about the people in them. Do you sometimes feel the way they do? Next time you feel lonely, ask yourself some questions. What can I do to help myself? Who can I talk to? Then find someone you trust, like a parent or a teacher. Tell them how you are feeling. Talking helps.

CALVIN'S STORY

Calvin was in his room. He gave his model plane a big push. It crashed into the dresser. Calvin threw himself on his bed. Bang! went the bed against the wall.

"Quiet!" shouted Calvin's big brother Josh. Josh was in the room next door, doing homework.

Calvin looked around his room.

"What can I do?" he thought. "I've read all my books. I've made my bed. I'm tired of my puzzles. I'm bored, bored, bored!"

He sighed. He put his hands in his pockets and went downstairs.

Calvin walked along the hall. He started to sing. Calvin had a special song for when he felt bored. It didn't have any words, and there wasn't much of a tune. But he sang very loudly.

"Pom, Pom, Pom," sang Calvin. He wandered through the house to the kitchen. "Pom, POM!"

"What a terrible noise!" said Calvin's mother. "You'll wake Ashley. Go outside and play."

Calvin sighed again. He walked down the sidewalk. As he went, he kicked at the grass along the edge. He watched the toes of his white sneakers turning green. Scuff, Scuff! went Calvin's feet. "Pom, Pom," he sang.

Soon a head popped out from under the car.
"Stop that awful noise, Calvin!" said his father.
Calvin gave a great big sigh. He sat down near the fence. He watched his father. He found a stick and ran it along the fence. Crick, Crick! went the stick.

Calvin sat and thought about his friends from school. He wondered what they were all doing.

"I wish I didn't live so far away from the other guys," he thought. And all the time he ran the stick along the fence. Crick, Crick, Crick!

How do you think Calvin feels right now?

"Calvin!" shouted his father after a while. "Put that stick down and come over here." Calvin dropped the stick and went over to his father.

"What's the matter?" his father asked.

"Nothing," said Calvin. "Well, there's nothing anyone can do about it, anyway."

"There's always something you can do—about anything," said his father. "What's the matter?"

"I'm bored," said Calvin. "I can't play with Josh because he's too old. And Ashley's just a baby. The guys at school don't live near here. I'm bored."

"It sounds to me like you're lonely," said his father.

He sat down next to Calvin and said, "Let's think of some ways you can make friends around here."

"They all know each other already," said Calvin quietly. "I don't count."

"It's no use just feeling sorry for yourself. You have to go out and make friends sometimes," his father said.

Then Calvin's father held up one hand.

"Five ways to stop feeling bored and lonely!" he said. He counted them off on his fingers.

"One! Join the soccer league. Two! Go hear the storytellers at the library. Three! Take swimming lessons at the park. Four! Invite someone to stay overnight. Five! Join the kids' choir at the community center."

What do you think of Calvin's father's ideas? Can you think of anything else Calvin could do?

Calvin's father looked proud of himself.

"Now, which do you want to do first?" he asked.

"Swimming lessons!" shouted Calvin. "And I'd like to have Bob over on Friday."

Calvin's father jumped up.

"Let's go, then," he said.

"Where are we going?" asked Calvin.

"To the park, to sign you up for those swimming lessons!" his father said.

At dinner, Calvin couldn't stop grinning.

"I'm taking swimming lessons every Monday after school," he told his mother. "And is it okay to ask Bob to sleep over on Friday night?"

"That's fine," his mother said, laughing. "Just don't teach him how to sing!"

How do you think Calvin feels now?

Feeling like Calvin

Sometimes it feels good to be on your own. There are all kinds of things that you can do by yourself. You can read, paint, make models, or listen to music. But it's fun to share with others too. Spending a lot of time by yourself can make you feel bored and lonely, like Calvin.

What can you do?

If you're feeling like Calvin, think what you can do to change things. Work out some ways to make new friends. Talk to kids at school. Make a list of other places where you might meet people—at a park, at a community center, at church. You could ask a parent or teacher to help you.

TRACY'S STORY

The children in Tracy's class were making a painting. They were making it together.

"This way, we can paint a really big picture," said Mrs. Lee, their teacher.

"How will we know what colors to use?" asked Lisa.

"You can take turns choosing colors," said Mrs. Lee.

"I'll go first!" shouted Joseph. "Let's do the sky. Let's paint it blue."

Soon, everyone had a paintbrush dipped in paint. They made a bright blue sky.

Tracy painted very slowly and carefully. She liked the feeling of the wet brush on the paper. She wanted to go faster, but she was worried that she might make a mistake. She was afraid that she might spoil the picture.

Every part of the sky had soon been painted. The children washed their brushes to get them clean. Then Mrs. Lee asked Hassan to choose a new color.

"Yellow," he said.

All the children dipped their brushes in yellow paint. Together they painted a huge yellow sun.

Then it was Lisa's turn. Lisa chose the color green. After Lisa came Philip. He chose red. Some children splashed the paint as they worked. Others dribbled it. But Tracy didn't make one splash or dribble. She was painting very, very carefully.

"It's your turn to choose a color now, Tracy," said Mrs. Lee. All the children looked at Tracy. But Tracy looked down. She didn't say anything. It was very quiet. Everyone was waiting.

Joseph wanted to get on with the painting.

"Tracy never knows!" he called. "I know! I know! Let me choose again!"

Mrs. Lee wouldn't let Joseph choose again.

"We'll wait for Tracy," she said. But Tracy couldn't think of any colors at all. Everyone was watching her. Tracy felt very small and lonely.

"I'm not like Lisa or Hassan or Joseph. I can't choose a color. I don't want a turn," thought Tracy.

Have you ever felt like Tracy does now?

"It's your choice, Tracy," said Mrs. Lee again. She sounded nice. Tracy looked at her teacher. She tried to forget about everyone else.

"Purple!" said Tracy at last.

"Purple!" said everyone. "That's just the color we need!" They all began painting with the thick purple paint.

Soon the painting was finished. Mrs. Lee taped it up. It stretched all along the wall. Tracy's class was very pleased with the painting.

"Tracy's purple is my favorite color!" said Joseph. Tracy smiled.

At the end of the day, everyone rushed toward the door. But Mrs. Lee stopped them.

"Wait! Hold up your hands, everyone!" she called.

They held their hands above their heads.

"That's what I thought," said Mrs. Lee. "You all have to wash your hands. They're covered in purple paint." Mrs. Lee laughed. "And guess whose are the messiest?"

"Mine!" said Tracy, smiling.

How did Tracy's teacher help? How do you think Tracy feels now?

Feeling like Tracy

Have you ever felt lonely, the way Tracy did? Tracy wasn't just shy. She felt that she was different from everyone else. She felt that she couldn't do what the others could do. She got used to that feeling.

Being brave

Loneliness is a sad feeling. Sometimes it's easier to be lonely than to join in. But you have to be brave. Think how brave Tracy was when she said "Purple!" It was hard at the time, but it made her feel great afterward.

You're not alone

It helps to remember that lots of people feel shy and lonely sometimes. You aren't the only one. And you can do something about it. Keep trying. Don't forget to help others too. If you think that someone else is feeling shy, how could you help them join in? What would you have done to help Tracy?

Feeling lonely

Think about the stories in this book. Tina, Calvin, and Tracy all felt lonely. They each found someone to help them. Tell a teacher or a parent how lonely you feel. They'll help you too.

If you are feeling frightened or unhappy, don't keep it to yourself. Talk to an adult you can trust:

- one of your parents or other relatives
- a friend's parent or other relative
- a teacher
- the principal
- someone else at school
- a neighbor
- someone at a church, temple, or synagogue

You can also find someone to talk to about a problem by calling places called "hotlines." One hotline is **Child Help,** which you can call from anywhere in the United States. Just call

1-800-422-4453

from any telephone. You don't need money to call.

Or look in the phone book to find another phone number of people who can help. Try

- Children and Family Service
- Family Service

Remember you can always call the Operator in any emergency. Just dial 0 or press the button that says 0 on the telephone.